MAGIC

IN

YOU

DR SUMANA CHAKRABORTY

First published in 2020 by

Becomeshakespeare.com

One Point Six Technologies Pvt Ltd.
119-123, 1st Floor, Building J2, B - Wing, WadalaTruck
Terminal, Wadala East, Mumbai, Maharashtra, India, 400022.
T:+91 8080226699

ISBN - 978-93-90543-25-0

Table of Contents

Introduction

I want to thank you and congratulate you for downloading the book **THE MAGIC IN YOU** – *A guidance to inner self.* This book contains proven steps and strategies on how to look at life situations in the most productive and fulfilling way, commonly known as being happy. I want to commend you for taking the first steps to venture into the world of self-empowerment.

Have you always dreamed of a world where you are respected, valued and have worth? Now is the time! Read through the next few pages to understand and learn about all the essential steps towards your life's success. I am looking forward to sharing with you the principles that have enabled so many people to convert their dream of being successful and happy with complete life balance into a reality.

We need knowledge and identification of self needs and fears that create an environment for a success road in order to battle out the uncertain social and environmental changes. Path breaking offerings by coaches and well-known influencers, in the form of quotations, sayings, proverbs and life examples, result in new living standards and comparisons, which can produce a cascading effect or virtuous circle in your lifestyle and livelihood. If we understand the benefits and drawbacks, a balanced approach to nurturing the knowledge and perceptive of experienced visionaries will definitely result in a positive impact on our life goals and society model.

With lively incidents and examples, this book explains every aspect of life, which should be molded and rightly looked upon to get a better version of one's own self in life.

This book would serve the readers at their best and be a life changing experience by which they would mold their life, and move forward on the road of life, making it to a beautiful destination ahead.

I'm excited to see how this information affects your life and hope to hear plenty of amazing success stories!

Thanks again for downloading this book, I hope you enjoy it!

"Being a human, you inherit having all the features of a human, a heart of humanity and the power of mind that can analyze and feel at a very high level of coherence. You are my child. I am a human and the only thing you inherit from me is being the human. The rest is up to you..."

Chapter 1: The Human

It was a hot summer afternoon. Sitting on a recliner chair, my grandma was irritably blabbering about having the right to give her acquired property to whomever she wishes and no one should have a say on the topic.

As a nine-year-old kid, the blabbering should not have made sense to me if it wasn't directed towards my mother. It was the first time that I heard of the words inheritance, will, property transfer and had a detailed discussion with my father that evening about inheritance - the handovers from one generation to another. Not that I understood much, yet my father always answered my questions in simplest ways possible and never tired of answering till I got distracted or tired of questioning. I was a full of questions child and my father was a full of answers dad.

That day my dad might have explained the need of a will or inheritance document, explained the related feud of inheritance of property, and much more; yet the only thought that stayed with me was the answer to one of my questions; What do I inherit from you, Bapi?

"Being a human, you inherit having all the features of a human, a heart of humanity and the power of mind that can analyze and feel at a very high level of coherence. You are my child. I am a human and the only thing you inherit from me is being the human. The rest is up to you…"

What have YOU inherited from your parents; lifestyle, house, car, bank balance… Have you inherited their features, characteristics, values or teachings?

Take a deep breath, and give it a thought.

What YOU get from your ancestors is what you are gifted. Their features, characteristics, lifestyle, beliefs all make an impact on your life. We all inherit something from our parents, which they inherited from their parents and maybe that's how the cycle goes on.

God created man in his own image, in the image of God he created him; male and female he created them.

-Genesis 1:27 ESV

HE, who created the world, saw his image in humans, but do You think, you have ever inherited any of his qualities yet?

If we dive into the dictionary-definition of the term 'inheritance', we can conclude that,

"Inheritance is all that you possess as your birth right from your parents as well as ancestors."

And each of us is a human due to the inheritance. The knowledge, property, lifestyle, fame, name, identity and social status are all choice handovers, yet the one thing that needs no extra effort and is as a handover since birth is being human. This is the one inherited character that goes most unnoticed and is never gratified for.

God-believers often say that they are the children of God, yet mostly forget to gratify their parents and ancestors for giving them this opportunity to be the child of God through inheritance of the ancestors.

In the Hindu custom, the head of a family has a ritual of praying and feeding the ancestors through a 15-day ritual during a particular time of year, yet nowadays rarely does anyone appreciate the essence of being gratified for the inheritance.

The next time you ask yourself what your parents left you with; look at yourself in mirror, the features of a HUMAN being is your inheritance and it is your responsibility to be behave humanely each moment of your life to honor the inheritance.

Identity is the fact of being who or what a person or thing is... In simple application it should be the answer to the question, WHO are YOU!!!

It takes a lifetime and the answer keeps changing, enhancing or even sometimes covered in silence.

How often do you meet a person who answers the question of identity as designated and documented in their birth certificate or states the names given by family and friends (society).

I am a winner/loser/lazy/smart/hardworking/callous (as many adjectives in a language and more). Adjectives are the identity of so many people. You too might be one of those who confuses habits, lifestyles, way of work or occupation and designation as their identity.

"THE MAP IS NOT THE TERRITORY!!!!"

While this is your place and identification as per society norms, that's it, changeable and essentially it isn't YOU!!

You inherited Humanity, and now you are what your eyes see, what your ears hear and what your brain interprets and perceives. While as humans you are social beings and all social norms apply to you, the society doesn't define you, you are to present yourself to society...

Next time, society asks you who you are, answer as per the person asking you the question and when you ask yourself in the mirror, make sure the answer never changes... Your identity is what you tell your mirror!! That is termed as character.

"Identity is a strange business; we spend our entire life earning one."

In the race of creating one,

YOU often forget to see yourself with your own eyes.

Does each human have the same perspective about a thing or event?

You have seen maps. You have access to google maps now, it represents an area so much in detail, it almost brings the impression of the place to your mind... ALMOST!!! Because what so ever advanced AI be used, you have to physically reach the place to see and feel and be in that place.

Hence THE MAP IS NOT THE TERRITORY!!!! The phrase was coined by Alfred Korzybski and has been in use in multiple psychological and sociological implications for years, yet stands correct for an eternity.

YOU are exclusive and so is your viewpoint, your perception and your narration of an event. You should know your identity and that should never be defined by any other, because the others can see you but can't BE YOU!!

How many times have you said to someone, 'this is personal', be it an answer that makes you uncomfortable, or someone intruding in your personal space by words, actions or body language.

If you are aware of the Proxemics rules and definitions, that is; the human use of space and its impacts on social interactions, behavior and communication, you can relate it to non-verbal communications. The leaders and influencers use non-verbal communication to make an impact and most commoners know it for sure when the proximity of an individual is permitted and when not.

Can you do the same for emotions?? You keep saying 'Personally, I feel....' yet isn't it redundant?? Because everything you feel is personal. While loads of others may empathize yet no other person can ever feel the same, not even if treated in the same way in the same situation as the feelings are exclusively yours and form the basis of your identity, shaping the story of your life..

You are an engineer by degree and now working at a handsome salary in an organization. There were 120 other classmates in your college and you joined with

12 of them in the organization and 5 joined the same project. And today, on your third worki-versary, you have the same mail sent to 3 from the same supervisor. If name was not in consideration, are all three of you the same?

While giving this a thought take a minute to remember when you followed suit to your predecessors, when each one had to introduce themselves.

"Name, qualification, designation, project name"

Sanjay Mitra, BE, Associate, XYZ

Ananya Rajan, BE, Associate, XYZ

Rajendranath, BE, Associate, XYZ

Quilcene, BE, Associate, XYZ

Doyouhaveaname, BE, Associate, XYZ…. So on…

The last two aren't names… yet none of them were introductions of the individuals, they are just data of the group seated at a meeting. You can find them in an excel!!

Next time anyone asks you to introduce yourself, do not follow suit of your predecessor as it's your introduction not theirs!!

YOU present and introduce yourself to the society, be it family, workplace or community. Feel free to say how to want to **introduce yourself in the best possible light**, keeping the norms of the place and integrity of the organizational or social standards in mind.

Re-read the above paragraph once more keeping the bold words in special attention. The identity you show to others should be meant to put you in the best possible light, no falsification, no blending or copying others and not based on other's opinions!!

The day you start this off and keep practicing this voluntarily, you will not need anyone to explain the meaning of personality, because you will have one to know it!!

Personality is a bunch of characteristics by which we define a person's, traits, beliefs, and values.

It is never too early or too late to start this practice and build as well as control your personality. Be it 15 years or 50, start off, and if you have already started, check and control your personality. If you think you are not a public figure and hence personality is not a concern for you, trash the reason immediately as while you talk to your son, you have a personality, when you talk to your peer you have a personality and when your colleague visits your home and talks to your parents, you have a personality. And if you haven't worked on it, you won't be eligible to blame anyone for an insult whereas if you build it, no one can break it and hence, you would never be insulted.

Remember, you deserve respect and you can have it without enough money in your pocket or high social standards. All you have to do is be respectful of others and build your personality. Again, start today, you had to do it yesterday, today you are one day late. Better late than never!!

Personification is the attribution of a personal nature or

human characteristics to something non-human, or the representation of an abstract quality in human form.

While personification is for non-humans, it is YOUR responsibility to never personify yourself, 'I am the sun, moon, earth, wall or wind'… Because while personification is needed for non-humans, it is lethal when used in reverse, especially for our brains which understands direct orders and behaves like a wall, confusing our conscious feelings and creating imbalance in emotions and life…

Yes, YOU are… Steady as a wall, disciplined and service-oriented like the sun, a light of hope in the darkness like the moon, calm and supportive like the earth and enthusiast like the wind…

Yet you aren't strong as the sun because the strength of the sun is a personification of the human attribute and you are stronger as you are strong just like YOU, the HUMAN!!

The most important is that each one of YOU is special and unique in their own way!

What do YOU leave behind, when you die?

You leave behind L E G A C Y.

Your attributes, achievements, as told by your successors and sometimes when your impact is beyond family, it is your legacy that the world/society remembers you for!!

While we all know some business owners and millionaires of the past, most of their legacy is not their company turnover or property papers, it is their vision, their impact and their life story.

You may gift your child all your property or nothing, yet your legacy is what your child and family will remember you for and that in turn depends on how well you tell your story, your story of life!!!

So, how good are you telling your story? Make sure it's good and your dear ones know your story, so you have a legacy…

Age has nothing to do with starting to build your life story, you don't need a successor to start your legacy. YOU create and maintain your legacy; the world only takes over... You are a living legend and you should build your exclusive story from day 1. Start your journey to the legacy today!!

Well, do remember, your legacy you leave behind yet no on inherits it... like you did not inherit your predecessor's legacy, you have them as handovers…!!!!

YOU are a legend and hence, all you need to do is start building the legacy!!

While all this sounds impressive, it sounds gibberish on a practical note, and that is where a coach comes to your rescue. A professional, who would set your mindset of individuality and help you see the path onward to your legacy that is in society terms, your SUCCESS!!!

Every individual needs a coach to reiterate the essence of individualism and set the path of life journey, so that as many times as YOU are taken off the road, you have the power to seek the map embedded in you to your goal and your legacy!!

A coach is a one time guide to bring you face to face with YOU!! The rest is simple because all YOU need is in YOU!!!!

Inheritance, identity, personality, and legacy, are the phases of a human life goal cycle.

You cannot escape any stage, as each phase is a lesson and a gift which You either receive or leave behind for some other You.

In the effort of defining the humans, even I am incapable of defining YOU, being YOU, writing about YOU to tell YOU that;

YOU are the most important person in your life.

And, thank you for being YOU…

"In society, YOU have been assigned a constant stage, if you don't present your show, your audience will create one of their liking and that will never be in your favor, so start the performance on your stage, mindful of each gesture, identity and words you present to your audience."

Chapter 2: Let the world know YOU

Dictionary says,

"A society is a group of individuals, created or formed for the common benefit of all."

Some believe society is the master!!

The society together sets a boundary around you, and when you try to go beyond it, it reminds YOU of those boundaries.

For the sustenance of society, its norms are necessary and for you to be its part, abiding to the basic rules are mandate too. Yet it is essential to understand that society doesn't decide your presentation of self to society, YOU do.

Tolerating and respecting the norms of social behavior is enough to be part of society. A perfect social person is a myth and should not be the aim of a HUMAN.

In order to be accepted by society, it is important to abide by it, whether You like it or not.

YOU may have the stage and script ready, but it is the society which tells you if you are capable of being on the stage or not.

Imagine YOU being on stage while the world is watching YOU as an audience and you are the MASTER OF YOUR OWN SHOW,

YOUR OWN LIFE,

YOU BEING YOUR MASTER!

.

.

.

YOU, a highly powerful individual.

P O W E R is the act of making a change with your actions.

If you have seen the movie, *Mera Naam Joker,* you understand that the joker (protagonist character), wasn't just paid to be a clown around the stage, but for the fact that his existence made a difference on the stage, in the lives of the audience and therefore, SOCIETY.

In another movie, Batman, The JOKER, an antagonist character, impacted so much in the lives of the other characters in the movie as well as the audience that, at a later date, an independent movie on the character was welcomed whole-heartedly.

While he was just playing his role, which YOU all have to in life, he was powerful enough to control others' mind as well as his own.

He made other's laugh, or be thoughtful, being in the deepest sorrow or serenity.

In society, YOU have been assigned a constant stage, if you don't present your show, your audience will create one of their liking and that will never be in your favor, so start the performance on your stage, mindful of each gesture, identity and words you present to your audience.

As the French Revolution spoke in the field of theatre and drama, people demand realism on stage from YOU; not YOU actually, but from the role that You are playing up on stage.

Each action has an opposite reaction; hence your actions define your place in the society.

The society applauds the YOU on the stage which is actually **NOT YOU**.

No one has to know the **real YOU,** how You are to your mirror. The preference you provide to your audience, be it family, friend or foe, it is to be considered carefully; like the ticket to a stage show.

Let's say you gave a front ticket (access to your secrets), to someone and the person ditched you, take the ticket back instantly and either keep to yourself or find another deserving person.

Are you the same manager at home or the same father at work. Your presentation changes as per your audience. It's a matter of practice and soon you traverse from showing personality to practicing lifestyle and finally to having a story, an identity for the society. And the best part is you can always change your script and your audience, which best suits you.

It might be difficult, yet it is necessary to prohibit access to people who hurt you, and is essential to keep

---

"Only the people who give adequate quality time to the rest period succeed faster and gain higher goals..."

---

the irritating yet beneficial person in the show, in front of the stage of life!!

There is always room for yourself in the backstage where it is essential to find time in-between shows to face the mirror. None of the audience (even parents, spouse or besties), can ever replace the backstage mirror. Diary writing is one of the common habits of accessing the backstage mirror.

Have you ever questioned yourself that;

Hey! Dear me, who you are?

How are you?

Do you have a dream?

Can you achieve it?

Are you happy with me?

Life never ends, the stage can never be left empty.

THE SHOW MUST GO ON!!!

Apart from a prep time in the backstage, where for about the first ten years of life, you might allow your guardian, yet after that it is you alone with your mirror which might be a diary, your mind or a journal…

You cannot leave the stage ever,

NEVER

I repeat, N E V E R…

You can just close the ticket counter, like in movies,

HOUSEFULL is allowed!!

SORRY, WE ARE CLOSED is not allowed!!

So, the break time becomes really important and as fate may have it, break time is given least importance by most people. Only the people who give adequate quality time to the rest period succeed faster and gain higher goals… not the performance on stage but the rest time makes you a winner on stage!!

From the poem Birches, by Robert Frost

"I'd like to get away from earth awhile

And then come back to it and begin over."

It simply means, you can close the ticket counter for a while and escape to your reel world of imaginations, but then come back to the reality of life, where YOU need to be YOU!

"That would be good both going and coming back.

One could do worse than be a swinger of birches."

YOU cannot hang in between two worlds, at the end YOU need to show the world the real YOU, know the real YOU, or else you fail as a human in life and in stage.

Be the real YOU,

The YOU, you want the world to know YOU by.

…

YOU can only act for some time, not a lifetime…

In the end, how will you face the mirror and tell YOU, that you are FAKE.

How will you live being a fake person and please everyone?

The world is not a wish granting factory, nor are you, *Aladdin's Jinn* that YOU can fulfil people's dreams. What YOU can do is fulfil **your own dream**, and tell the world who **YOU** are, and what YOU are.

So that one day, even the world can thank you and say,

Thank you for being

YOU,

JUST YOU.

Chapter 3: Impact of Voice

In the dictionary, the word voice is always defined twice:

1. the sound produced in a person's larynx and uttered through the mouth, as speech or song.

2. a particular opinion or attitude expressed.

While the first one is voice physiologically, the second one is opinionated!!!

Let's start with the first one. Most of us are blessed with a proper functioning larynx and with the power of speech, we have a chance of enhancing by means of words and language, wrapped in emotions and voice modulations to make sure we communicate properly.

There are changes in our voice as per our emotions - serious, funny, happy, sad, excite or bored... The voice changes, sometimes even the accent changes.

Realization and utilization of these voice modulations forms a firm tool in communications.

There is a Chinese proverb, "The tongue can paint what the eyes can't see."

V O I C E is a powerful organ gifted by God to help YOU speak what YOU want to, what YOU feel and want to convey.

In simple words, VOICE is the power and ability to speak.

A hoarse voice when you are crying is a perfect example of how your voice indicates your inner feelings about the content and context.

That brings us to the second definition of voice, opinion…

There's a voice of OPINION which flows in each human that allows YOU to distinguish between what is right and wrong, or raise an argument for what YOU believe is right or wrong.

This voice is not the one which can be subjugated under the power of money, social status, your age or gender. A voice is something that is free to all, just like the eyes which are not restricted or subjugated by these, it sees what it sees, So is YOUR OPINION.

The voice is what enhances knowledge and helps You learn new things leading to self-development.

The voice of knowledge is one of the most powerful things to spread.

If YOU ever notice, it is some people's ability to speak what they feel that makes them so powerful that You look up to them and trust their words for the way they say it, you feel it's right.

Voicing out brings change in the society, be it women empowerment, girl education, acceptance of LGBT community, or depression, each and every

---

"Unless you voice and express yourself, no amount of change can be made, YOU are the society You wish to see a change in."

---

change witnessed its own revolution which was the result of the opinions, judgements being raised by them.

Unless you voice and express yourself, no amount of change can be made, YOU are the society You wish to see a change in.

There is a thin line between opinion and belief... Opinion is your perception about an ongoing event and you should always share it. Beliefs are self-fulfilling prophecies; they serve power for you and create distress in society if combined to the perception of an event.

ANYTHING is rightfully true to you if you believe it to be, that is not your opinion... Opinion is the way you see ANYTHING, a narration from your perception, that's all...

Consider the difference diligently so that you share your opinion and keep your beliefs to yourself.

The bright summer day in the busy city of Kolkata had no impact on the gloomy and serious couple, sitting in the waiting room of a congregate care center, willing to have a child of their own, so as to provide one child from the center with the happiness of a parent's love and happiness the exhilarating feel of parenthood themselves.

The care center always found ways to encourage family acceptance for the children in the center, because their core belief was the need of love and care of a family that shapes the character and influences the future of a

---

"Beliefs are self-fulfilling prophecies."

---

kid. Though the center did its best in providing basic health, food, education and care needs, the essence of a parent and family could never be matched.

This adoption case was a bit different, hence the seriousness and gloomy mood in the room. Usually the birth of a child was unknown to the center and religion and customs followed by all the children were based on Hinduism, with knowledge and acceptance of other religions like Islam and Christianity, so that whatsoever the family of adoption be, the customs, caste or birth parentage wouldn't matter, and also, rarely would any child be there till age of 10 or 15 without being adopted. Most of the adolescent children were always a part of the center and were either sent forth for an individual future or were bound to the institution's work and care.

This morning, the child being considered was sent to the orphanage at the age of 6 years, due to the death of her parents. Saina was an active child since day 1 and after an initial hiccup of dealing with the tragedy, she was an adorable stern Muslim kid, who observed her rituals and respected all other customs and festivities of the center. She was a friend to all because of her amicable nature and bright mind. She was a 9-year-old now, three years in this care center. Unlike other kids, she had a birth identity, knew her birth parents and had an absolute belief in the customs that she followed.

Ideally, she should have been open for Muslim parents only, yet her upbringing in this care center had been of tolerance and mixed culture, with humanism on top of all customs, hence, she was today being considered by a Hindu couple for adoption. The tension in the room gave a clear indication of an imbalance or indecision.

While the couple found Saina beautiful and well-behaved, Mrs. Kapoor had found out about her caste just an hour ago and this is not setting well with her belief system. There were numerous conflicts in her mind, Namaaz and Chants in same house, how would I manage my worship rituals? What face to show after death in heaven? And mostly, **what would people say?**

Mr. Kapoor, in a confusion to find a manageable balance in adoption of Saina and maintaining his wife's peace of mind, planned to ask Saina to change her religion and her name to Sneha. He believed that a kid of 9 years wouldn't be rigid in her belief system.

When Saina was called and asked the same question, whether would she change her religion to get a family, she asked politely, 'Will you allow me to pray to my God?'

That's an easy one, thought Mrs. Kapoor, and replied instantly, 'Yes, obviously. We have so many gods in Hinduism, choose any and worship, or worship all of them, no one will ever forbid you from prayers. Chants, rituals, customs, we are full of it in our house, a room for gods only. We have early morning prayers, feed god before our food and evening prayers as well. You can have your own takshaal (seat for chanting), if you wish so.'

Hearing all of it, Saina lowered her face and sadly replied, 'My god just needs a few minutes of heartfelt prayer on a clean mat facing eastward early in the morning at sunrise and optionally 4 more times in a day. While I would love to pray to all gods and seek blessings, I cannot leave my god to have my parents!!'

The clear opinion of a nine-year-old kid left the beliefs of the much aged adults dumfounded.

This is based on a real time situation that has happened in front of my eyes and have helped distinguish the power of opinion while abolishing the need to propagate one's belief. What happened to Saina, whether she got a family of her choice and how successful she has been in her studies and career are out of scope of this chapter and discussion.

A major takeaway is that once we differentiate between opinion and belief, we make space for all in society and none in ourselves. An this is the essence of maintaining self-belief while making space for all in human society and community.

It's just the matter of opinion, even amongst thousands of opinions she chose to speak her opinion without the fear of being rejected. She took the risk of losing a family, a good future for she could not sacrifice her morals.

Education gives the power to explore more, and know what is right and wrong. If a person is educated it doesn't mean he/she is superior and has the right to take decisions. KNOWLEDGE is always the real power a human holds and Opinionizing your knowledge, your beliefs is way too important than any degree or experience.

Your opinion might be right or wrong, but YOU need to respect it, for the fact that it is what YOU think.

That's how YOU can create an impact with YOUR VOICE.

If YOU cannot raise your opinion, be it good or bad, how will YOU ever grow as a human being in life?

Your opinion can change and always make an impact, just that YOU have to express it.

If YOU want a happy ending, you have to create a happy start and maintain a happy journey.

It's YOU who can make a difference,

It's always YOU,

And, it will always be YOU.

Chapter 4- Word Your Voice

God has given you the power to speak, will you mute it? When God has given you the sword of education, will you rust it?)

Let's have a look at the definition of Language in the dictionary... 'The method of combining your words which is as vocal as your actions to express your ideas and beliefs is what a language is.'

"Language is the expression of ideas by means of speech-sounds combined into words. Words are combined into sentences, this combination answering to that of ideas into thoughts." – Henry Sweet.

Language is a medium of communication, and English is just ONE of the languages to communicate and express yourself. Each language has its own power if used diligently and consciously.

Food has always been a moment of togetherness for all families, it knows no boundaries. nor are bhajias just for people who speak Hindi, nor is Pizza just for people speaking English. If we are to believe the food experts, tastes and foods have a language of their own...

Aarti, the simple Marathi house helper of a modern, foodie Hindi/English - speaking family was responsible for cooking food and caring for the kids during the office hours of the couple of the house.

'Ek tohfa se nawaaza hai khuda ne tujhe,
Kya usse sirf maa kehne mein gawa doge,
Ek taalim ki taakat di hai usne,
Kya usse yuhi bewajah gawa doge?'

-self-musing, Dr. Sumana

In contrast to traditional food habits of Aarti, her employer's family was fond of cuisines like Italian, Mexican, Thai, Chinese, Mughlai and so on.

Aarti was a good cook, yet these modern cuisines were a mess as the recipes were not available easily and most of the spice combinations didn't follow traditional rules, making the work in her new job a challenge. She had the magic of great taste in traditional food and was naïve in modern diversified foods.

Times had changed. Pasta, pizza, ravioli, Mexican rice and such dishes ruled the taste buds now. After having a day's struggle with herself, she managed to gather courage and approach the housemaker, Mrs. Sharma, to reveal her lack of knowledge in cooking pasta, pizza and other modern delicacies. While Mrs. Sharma found it odd that the cook didn't know how to cook delicacies of their choice and the added challenge irritated her enough to sack Aarti, yet her frank acceptance in a tone to learn made her consider that she is a genuine person who cares a lot for her children, hence deserves a chance to learn the needed recipes to cope.

So, Mrs. Sharma gifted Aarti a new phone with an internet connection, and taught her how to use YouTube, so that she could watch the recipe in Hindi, and learn to cook. Being a fast learner, it took Aarti about a fortnight to master the basics of pizza, Momo, noodles, and also, the kid's favorite, pasta. Not that she could name the ingredients or understand any variant names, yet she prepared good food by visual learning of techniques and ingredients.

She was not dependent on the English language to prove her sincerity, skills as a chef and loyalty to work.

Language is a medium to communicate and make understanding better. It has no barriers or restrictions, it just needs to be understood.

...

LANGUAGE is organized for reappearance of events and utilization of the knowledge to be transferred. Meaningfulness, arbitrariness and openness forms the essence of language, essentially forming a sound meaning link.

The two same words in the same language can be in different order to propose different meanings and seem like different messages to the listener!

The situation being a grandfather came to visit, and the mother saying these words with the grandchild sitting beside the grandfather!!

- Child, kiss grandfather- The child is being asked to kiss the grandfather.

- Grandfather, kiss child- The grandfather is being asked to kiss the child.

- Kiss grandfather, child! – The child is being commanded to kiss the grandfather.

- Kiss child, grandfather! – The grandfather is being commanded to kiss the child.

COMMUNICATION is passing of information from one to another by using:

- Signals
- Transmitter
- Channel receiver

Signals - Words, gestures and body language form the signals, Transmitters. Interest, common grounds and intent form transmitters. Channel receiver - Visuals, audio and emotions form the channel receivers.

The easier this seems to point out, the more complex it becomes on application, yet a few basic rules of communication rule every room of individuals.

When it comes to communication with others, we rely on the most sophisticated human skill - Language.

Humans communicate through other forms of language as well, as explained in the example called Paralanguage.

Paralanguages are expressed in the form of:

1. Voice Pitch/ Tone
2. Proxemics
3. Body Language
4. Eye Contact
5. Gestures
6. Actions
7. Visual Images

As an individual, what YOU must have is a good vocabulary to convey your voice into words…

Some suggestions to help you inculcate a good command over words are:

- Know the different meanings of words you speak (keep a dictionary handy even for your native language.)

- Use every opportunity to speak in front of family and friends, speak out, give your opinions, just express yourself. It will make YOU more active in learning new words and their inner meanings.

- Generate curiosity to know what you hear and question people to explore new thoughts and beliefs.

Communication is the essence of human survival, be it by your mouth, gestures, eye contact, actions, body language or anything. It just should be able to convey your thoughts, YOU matter, so do your thoughts and opinions.

YOU all have to voice out your beliefs and learnings, or gain knowledge or reach out your knowledge into the minds of other YOU.

In the end, YOU have to Voice YOUR Words,

Your Thoughts,

Your Opinions,

AND

Yourself.

Chapter 5: Know Your Friends to have a Great Friendship

When I was young, we used to say a line about friendship, "Friendship is a ship which never sinks." As I advanced in life and had some bitter sweet experiences that my journey had to offer, I understood the gravity of this line. Friendship, is actually the ship, which does not sink. A popular theory broadly distinguishes between friendships of two kinds; one is a genuine friendships and the other two kinds are friendships based on mutual usefulness and on pleasure.

The above stated theory can be very well identified in the modern world. These days, the younger generation has categorized their friendships into various types, movie friends gym/morning walk friend, shopping friend, study buddy and many more such types. These types of friendships fall under the category of 'Friendship based on mutual usefulness or pleasure'. Basically, you remember such friends only when you are in certain setting or surrounding. A gym/morning walk friend cannot be your shopping friend, because apart from your interest for fitness nothing else matches. Similarly, your study buddy might not be your movie companion, again due to lack of similar taste.

Exception to all above list, the '3 AM Friend' is mostly a friend whom you have known practically for almost the whole of your life and has only a way into your life,

"Friendship is a ship which never sinks."

never out. This friend not only knows you and your family in and out but also has been part of every phase of your life and seen your extremes. This I would say is 'Friendship.'

This friend is available always with you, at every moment, in all circumstances yet goes almost unnoticed; your self-confidence, self-respect, self-compassion and self-company.

Every time you see no other human, these stay and all you need is to befriend them.

So are each of your values; kindness, punctuality, charm and many others, who aid you in your work and are taken for granted. So, the next time you blame your friend of taking you for granted, remember these friends whom you take for granted, acknowledge and make use of them so that you can be a better friend to another person and have excellent friendships.

Not every friend we come across in our childhood stays in our life and becomes a part of our journey. As we grow, few drift away. Reasons are many, change of schools, change of neighborhood, change of city or even country, selection of different streams, which leads to admission in different colleges. Also, as we grow and get exposed to different surroundings, we let new people in our life. Being a human tendency, new always attracts and we often take the old for granted, same happens with friendships too. We start spending more time with new friends in order to get them know more and since they share our academic (mostly) interests, we have more than one thing in common with them.

In spite of all these happenings in life, a few friends do stay. Lucky if we have them in our life and luckier if we are the one! The reason because of which they stay is, subconsciously, they both know, they are there for each other, always. As they say, side by side or miles apart, true friends are always connected by heart. Days might pass without a conversation or even a text, but it's only a matter of a phone call and it feels like they have just picked up from their last conversation.

Be it 3 am friend, movie companion, gym/morning walk friend, shopping friend, study buddy, each of them is important and plays a vital part in our well-being. A single person cannot play the all the roles and can't be omnipresent, hence, all of them have their own importance. It's true, nothing can replace a genuine friendship, but at times when our chaddi-buddy cannot make it, the shopping friend can uplift our mood just by being there. Hence, 'har ek friend zaruri hota hai.'

When a child is small, family is everything for him/her. Everything they experience, like going to the park, school, music or sport classes, picking up a fight with fellow children, etc, are shared with their parents or elder sibling. When the child grows, 8-10 years of age, the feeling of being an individual strikes, they no more want their parents or siblings to be put in the loop for each and everything they do. A sense of secretiveness crops up and the child starts thinking he/she should not be considered a kid anymore and hence, they do not want to involve their parents in their problems. This is where friendships bloom. A childhood friend, who was just a playmate or a classmate, now becomes your most trusted confidante and sometimes even a partner in crime.

For a child this is a very beautiful transition, friends metamorphosing into bosom friends. Here begins a safari, a beautiful and wild one, which both of them would cherish for their life, whose memories would cheer them up in gloomiest of times and whose impressions would always keep the child in them alive. So many, rather most of the firsts are experienced in this enthralling journey, first cycle ride out of the neighborhood, first pizza treat without family, first friendship day and the importance of friendship band, first crush, first heartbreak, first night out, first sleepover, first tuition bunk, so many firsts to list down, but each one very special.

They say all good things come to an end, well not necessarily, but yes, all good things do remodel as time goes by. There comes a time when even best of friends have to move on their individual paths which are different from each other. Here, the testing times begin for them and their friendship.

When a person becomes an inseparable part of your life, there sure comes a dependency factor. And it is not equal, there's always a person who is more dependent on the other comparatively. As long as they are together, it does not matter but when life happens, things change. One of the friends has to move out first and in case if he is the depended, it makes things really difficult for the other one. Despite of all the promises and commitments, it becomes difficult to have the same kind of friendship. As c mentioned earlier, the relationship is remodeled. In the flux, the friends who were naïve and childlike, always clinging to each other, suddenly transform into understanding and matured individuals, accepting that there is life beyond their friendship, but they are inextricable a part of each other's life, another beautiful metamorphosis.

Here, I would like to share small story. This story is of two young girls, one is very outgoing, chilled out daring, let's call her 'S'. The other was very sincere, studious, not very open, and kind of paranoid, let's name her 'N'. So, N and S met in the stupidest way possible but it was just the beginning of their life long wildest safari. Though they both belonged to different schools and later different colleges (even streams), they were inseparable. They saw all the possible ups and downs together and stood by each other. It was difficult to say who was more dependent on whom, but they never thought they could be separated. But then life happened. 'N' had to leave the city to pursue higher career goals. They promised each other daily calls and Skype calls once in a week, but life took over their promises and slowly distance started creeping in, or so they thought. With some introspection and lots of nostalgia, the two girls bridged all the gap and even with miles of distance were close to each other as ever and how!

There are no set rules or guidelines for friendship, but few pointers which definitely work for everyone and every friendship:

Never judge your friends.

How much ever close you are to your friend, give him/ her their own space.

If you don't like something or have some issues, resolve them in person when the two of you are alone. Never put your friend in spot amongst other people, even if they are your closest friends.

Clear out misunderstandings as soon as possible.

You two may not share interests, still respect the other person's choice. Being a friend doesn't give you the right to make fun of the other person's choices.

Money has spoiled greatest of relationships, try not to involve money in your relationships.

Each person has certain limitations and tolerance, also each one has a soft spot which better not be messed with. Set boundaries, it's better not to indulge in a conversation which is not comfortable for another person.

Keep secrets of your friends, religiously.

Never interfere in their family matters unless asked. Lending a listening ear would suffice.

Even if the other person is just your movie buddy, never tell him or make him feel the same. You never know what importance you hold in their life.

Muhammad Ali has rightly said, "Friendship is the hardest thing in the world to explain. It's not something you learn in school. But if you haven't learned the meaning of friendship, you really haven't learned anything."

"Friendship is the hardest thing in the world to explain. It's not something you learn in school. But if you haven't learned the meaning of friendship, you really haven't learned anything."

Life is a celebration of love, togetherness and fulfilment. This celebration becomes more fun and cheerful when our friends accompany us. Have friends, lots of them but make sure you treasure the real ones, your 3 am friends.

Cheers to friendship!

Chapter 6: Hike in Worth

Survival is the essence of life…

No matter how much YOU struggle in life or beyond, in the end all YOU need to learn and do, is to S U R V I V E.

And,

Can YOU survive without a job?

Without money?

Without food?

Without a life?

NO right?

Another question where YOU might differ…

Can YOU survive without knowledge?

Without having a worth?

To be precise,

Without self-worth?

YOU all may have different answers to this, or approach. But there is no survival without a Job agreed, but nor is there any survival without self-worth.

If YOU don't know your worth, Feel YOU are important, how will YOU tell the world that,

YOU ARE IMPORTANT.

...

"Job is a regular duty assigned to a person for which he may or may not receive a fixed remuneration."

Hence, it is the basis of survival for human life as a job is the one which keeps life lively and adds a motive to life.

Job isn't just for money, job of being a son/ daughter, father/mother, husband/wife, employer/employee, boss/ staff; at each stage YOU fulfil your responsibilities and duties towards your job.

Talking about job, there is another term without which the word job seems of less value, i.e.,

DESIGNATION.

"Designation is a name or title added before a job, which makes it valuable and creates your identity."

In any job, especially monetary ones, designation plays a very important role in a human life as it creates their identity and also gives them a designated place in society. The term position has always mattered to society, to define a person's ability and skills.

A major difference between designation and knowledge, is that Designation defines your power and your identity, but knowledge defines you as a human, what you have learnt or experienced in life.

If you ask that is a designated person knowledgeable or not, I may think twice before answering, i.e., there might be a conflict of opinions, but where the question arises does a knowledgeable person always get a higher designation in life, it's not always true.

For example, in life, like in school you might have seen that a kid of class 4 or 5 might speak better English, or has more skills and knowledge than a class 8 or 9 boy. Even though he has supreme knowledge than the class 4 boy and high designation in school, doesn't mean he has more knowledge.

Designation can only give you an identity, but not the required knowledge for it.

YOU may earn Rs.200000 per month yet know nothing or have no interest in what You are doing, and YOU may earn Rs.25000 per month but love your job.

H I K E is something which is a need of the designated positioned and salaried men. For To survive and get appreciation both must hand in go hand so as to boost your morale.

"Hike simply means to get a raise or more than what you got."

The term more, does the job and makes people do theirs.

When a person possesses a skill, what they want from the world is appreciation of their talent or skill. So, is in a job and designation. YOU need recognition at each step to get zeal and energy to work further and work better.

Promotion is always a word used to excite a person. Promotion in every post is necessary for the cycle of life to work smoothly. With each step and time span, a promotion or rise is important.

More than important, it's a NEED.

A need of a human, to survive and live and feel important and valued.

Let's get clearer…

Roshan being a hardworking guy, who was the masters of finance, had a dream to work in a good office one day, and make his dad proud. Being a farmer's son, the pressure was too much and the road wasn't that easy. The most beautiful quality that he possessed was sincerity and loyalty. He was a satisfied soul guy, who was happy with whatever he had.

Isn't loyalty also a practice to be developed and practiced amongst humans?

Afterall,

Not everyone has it.

In the race of life and in temptation, he lost it all.

He started as an employee in the Kothari & Sons Co. and was very confident with his skills and knowledge being a scholar throughout his life. His starting salary was Rs.15000/ per month which was quite decent. His salary was not the concern for him any day, for he knew if he worked hard, he would succeed.

What he was concerned about was the fact that his friends, who didn't even work half as hard as him, were getting promoted, but he wasn't. He wanted to know where he lacked and they succeeded.

Upon asking his friends, the reason they told him was that they were helping the manager with his insight work, in return of which the manager promised to grant them a promotion and a hike of more than 15%.

Hearing this, at first, Roshan was astonished and said himself, he would never do so, but later upon watching his friends new lifestyle, he wanted to have the same. So, he made up his mind and asked the manager that he would do the same like others to him, if he promised a hike and promotion.

The manager agreed, and Roshan being great with numbers, started doing manipulation with his skills. Soon, he also got promoted, and got a 40% hike in his salary with the designation of Junior Manager.

Earning the position, his treachery grew more than ever, and he continued doing the manipulation, and in just 2 years, he became the Senior Manager, although he didn't have those skills at that point yet.

The fact lies that Roshan wasn't ready to wait to earn his position with the knowledge he had, he lost to the trap of an early promotion, when he didn't deserve it, at that point.

Success was one thing he wanted, but the road to it changed for him.

What is to be analyzed is that sometimes we lose our

worth to money, hike and designations to define our worth in the eyes of society. This was exactly what Roshan ended up with, his 5 years of degree and knowledge lost in the battle to the greed of hike in job and designation in life to achieve his goal.

His morale lost to promotion, and his skills to temptation.

Do YOU think Roshan got the salary hike owing to his skill or knowledge?

NO.

He got it because he agreed to use his knowledge to do something wrong just to earn a promotion in his job which he could never leave later making it a habit.

(How to know your self-worth Author insert here)

The only difference between the word fact and worth is of morale and ethics.

Fact may be ethical or not, but worth is always based on value which is pure.

Don't YOU think if Roshan would have used his same knowledge wisely, he would have been sucessfully, promoted as well as WORTHY.

YOU have to know your worth, different from what your job decides for you or society does.

YOU have to set,

YOUR STANDARD,

YOUR POSITION

YOUR VALUE

YOUR WORTH,

And, YOURSELF, in the society.

And, before asking for a hike in salary, upgrade yourself a little and

NAIL YOUR WORTH FIRST!

Chapter 7: Practice is the key to unlock a skill

A child when learns to walk, he doesn't start walking immediately.

At first, he crawls, falls a thousand times and then he learns to take baby steps and one day, he finally starts running and dancing on his own toes.

Each process needs time, just like a car needs each spare part to run, YOU need a lot of practice in everything YOU do to achieve a skill.

To explain better, let's take YOU back to your childhood.

In school, YOU might have noticed that the person with more responsibilities owns more skills as well as more friends.

Mohit, the guy of 11th standard, who was eager to be in class 12 to become the Head Boy of the school, a prestigious moment, right? He wanted to win at any cost so he started going to the gym to get stronger than his only strong competitor, Shubham.

Shubham was a popular guy in school as he was a great guitarist, dancer, debater, singer, as well as good in sports and academics. He had a huge friend circle in school as he was part of various clubs and used to practice them all diligently but never compromised on his studies. He knew he was weak in maths and therefore, he used to solve maths problems every day for at least 2 hours.

YOU can hire someone to show their skill for YOU but can YOU expect someone else to practice the skill on behalf of YOU?

-H. Jackson Brown Jr.

At the end, the criteria for being the head boy was to be decided by 25% based on academics, 25% by sports round and 50% on votes by the students.

As a result, the academics section was won by Shubham since he practiced mathematics each day as well as never compromised on studies while Mohit forgot everything in just concentrating on the gym to be better at sports.

The sports round was won by Mohit as he had practiced hard for it, which showed its result.

And the voting round was won by Shubham since he had a great network in school, as he had a number of skills as well as a great number of friends to vote for him.

Hence, we see that practice is indeed the master skill of human life. Understand that initiation of skills is a necessary quality for YOU to grow further in life and connect to the other YOU in life.

Even before you possess a talent, you have to make people believe that you can have that skill. The greatest mantra cycle of initiation of skill and for life is:

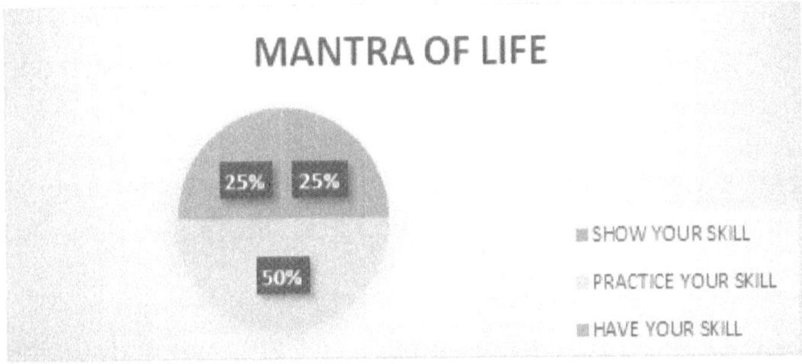

That's how YOU should target your skills i.e.

- Show Your Skill
- Practice Your Skill (or Perform Your Skill)
- Have Your Skill

So that at each step YOU know what to do and how to do.

In the field of practice of skills, knowing just WHAT TO DO isn't enough, HOW TO DO is also a matter of concern.

Let's understand with an example.

Radhika has always been a fat chubby girl who was known for her bubblish nature. When she was 6 years old, she used to shake her *kamariya* on songs like *kajra re kajra* and *Anarkali disco chali*. She had a very good knowledge on dance forms and every day she used to learn about new dance forms from the internet. Even during her school rehearsals, she used to observe dancers and their steps.

She had a very good eye on dance and therefore, could easily catch people's mistakes just like a teacher would. Being insecure of her weight, she hesitated to dance, and thought people would make fun of her but still she had the dream of dancing.

Her school dance teacher, Ms. Neha, saw the urge of dancing in Radhika and asked her what's stopping her from dancing.

She said with a low voice, "Ma'am, when I dance

everyone laughs at me because I am fat and not flexible like Sneha and the other dancers."

Neha said, "All these are just excuses, mere excuses. You don't even want to try hard before giving up. Look at me, I am 85 kgs still I dance and I am the teacher. If I would have lost hope would I ever be able to dance? Just get up and start dancing. Show your friends you can do it, and before that show it to yourself, be confident. Be flexible, be a dancer."

Hearing this Radhika got a boost, and decided to practice dance every day and get flexibility.

From the very next day, she started waking up at 4 in the morning and practiced for 2 hours from 4-6 each day and tried to do warm up exercises, new forms of dancing, and within a year, she was one of the best dancers of her school. She won the award for best dancer in her school, and showed her friends she was a dancer now.

But she didn't stop here, for her aim was not just to show her friends, but to dance, do what she loves. She started learning more new forms, creating her own fusion style dance forms and soon took part in the-school, state followed by national level dance competitions. By the age of 21, she became a successful dancer and opened her own dance academy and became a renowned choreographer.

She didn't stop, or leave practicing a single day. Even today, at the age of 56, she gets up at 4 and practices dance for 2 hours as well as teaches in her dance academy. It is something she never gets tired of, and has become a part of her life. She feels INCOMPLETE the day she doesn't dance, or teach her students.

…

This is the power of practice and also patience. YOU may not achieve something suddenly, but gradually YOU start achieving that a little more each day with effective and concentrated practice of your skill.

Virat Kohli, the captain of Indian Cricket Team, even today practices cricket each day. That is the level of dedication YOU need to show and PRACTISE HARD EACH DAY.

PRACTICE IS THE KEY,

TO ACHIEVE YOUR SKILLS!

TO CREATE AN IMPACT!

TO SUCCED IN LIFE!

TO BE PASSIONATE!

TO BE TALENTED!

TO BE YOU…

Chapter 8: Personality Awareness

'YOU are defined by the society on the basis of your features, characteristics, behavior by a word called P E R S O N A L I T Y.'

Personality is one of the strongest qualities a human possesses, which defines a person's existence in the society and the way people behave with them.

What we like in another person is all a reflection of their personality.

YOU like popular personalities; Sachin Tendulkar, Amitabh Bachchan, Alia Bhatt and others for the kind of hard work and performance they do. Their aura becomes a charm for others to admire and follow for the fact, that they are strong personalities, who represent themselves freely and we get charmed by the qualities they possess.

In your life as well, there are many personalities around YOU, whom You admire and learn from. If we like someone for the kind of person they are, that's what their personality is.

BUT

BUT

BUT

Again, a question…

Is a personality always positive?

If someone says, 'I want to become like Salman Khan."

Can't there be someone who says, 'I want to be like Ritesh Deshmukh of Ek Villan movie'?

Personalities are not always good; each human possesses some good and some negative features. Like some people learn about being greedy, selfish, criminal, terrorist being inspired with someone else's personality.

Just like Sachin Tendulkar is the GOD of cricket to many, Vijay Mallya maybe GOD to many.

YOU cannot control what someone likes in someone else or possesses, and sometimes not even know if what they are possessing is right or wrong.

Gods have always been praised for having a fascinating personality which each human wishes to acquire.

Lord Krishna, the one who used to steal maakhan from other's house in fun and innocence of course. If today a child does the same, will the society and people also laugh it out as his/her innocence or directly accuse saying he has no manners and is a thief? Will you accept if today a child in a playful mood of course, steals your daughter's clothes while she is bathing, again just for fun?

NO,

NO,

NO…

It's not about whether he was bad or he was good, it's about even he has multiple personalities. We need to admire the fact that each person has done some right and some wrong in their life. No one is perfect or can ever be, for there is no definition of perfection.

Another strong personality we all wish to be like is Lord Rama. The one who was so obedient that he went to 14 years of exile just because his father said so.

In a practical approach of life, do you even think the phrase, Pran jaaye par vachan na jaaye is applicable? Or, should be? Was it right to spend 14 years in a cave just for the sake of a promise, which even the one who gave didn't want to happen later?

We all have multiple personalities, so do Gods and everyone around YOU!

If YOU have seen Ramayana or heard the story, YOU all know Maa Sita was not accepted by Rama later on just because a dhobi said to him, that Maa Sita is apavitra.

Lord Rama himself knew he said wrong, after all Maa Sita wasn't even in the house of Raavana in reality, she was with Agni Dev.

The personality of that dhobi over powered the king himself, who being helpless let Sita out of the Mahal into the jungle all alone. The Maa Sita who gave her entire life to Lord Rama, spent 14 years in exile, suffered so much, but never accepted just because of the opinion of a dhobi.

It was just not an opinion, but an opinion said with a lot of confidence, that made it sound true, even when the dhobi himself just made an assumption. It was his personality that led the entire kingdom to believe his words.

Here, we can clearly see how a powerful person's personality, irrespective of their social status, power, position, a person's opinion and personality can lead to a great change. Maa Sita, who was such a strong personality didn't even once argue or ask her right to Rama and went to the jungle all alone. She didn't even care to remove the accusation put on her, just because she didn't want to or lost to the statement of a dhobi.

Lord Rama, the king, instead of telling his people what was wrong or right, with the aim of pleasing each individual of his kingdom, let go of Sita with his own eyes, and then regretted it for the rest of his life…

Wasn't it just the game of one personality, over all others?

….

If we talk about humans, do we really know ourselves?

Do YOU as yourself know your personality?

If I ask YOU to define YOU, can you do that?

Are we even aware of our features, qualities, traits, skills?

Do we really know ourselves, other than what others define us as?

If by chance,

YES,

Then do we really know where we want to lead ourselves as a human being in life, what good or bad we want to do with our personality to bring a change in our life and in others.

A human being must have a plan to utilise all he/she has, to lead to a final destination, and to do that you need to know yourself.

Suppose if YOU know, YOU are an introvert, you need to plan your goals accordingly and choose an aim that fits your personality like an office job and so on, or change your personality as per your goals. That's how a human grows.

Nobody is born talented, the ones who do debates, public speaking are not born confident, or not perfect in everything, but they gradually learn to speak and that's how they become fearless, and gain confidence.

Confidence is one of the assets to your personality, upon which your life depends.

It's either your way or the highway!

That exactly should be your approach towards your aim and develop a personality of this kind to achieve something.

The most important kind of freedom is to be what you really are.

-Jim Morrison

That's exactly how YOU need to be.

Among multiple personalities, one may fade after another, but what stays is YOU,

Your OWN PERSOANLITY,

YOU YOURSELF!

Before introducing yourself to the world, introduce yourself to yourself…

It's your identity, in the race of a million, YOU are one of the million, and there is no one like YOU,

WILL NEVER BE,

CAN NEVER BE,

SHOULD NEVER BE…

Just like a skill, YOU need to know how to:

· Know Your Personality

· Show Your Personality

· Practice Your Personality

· Have or Develop Your Personality

And, at the last, balance it all, because it's the essence for your survival.

Balance is one trait, which makes life easy, and meaningful. One cannot just focus on one thing or relation his/her entire life; the true art of a human is in framing each relation beautifully just like they how to keep in a family photo frame.

Can a human survive without having a personality of his own?

Absolutely not!

YOUR PERSONALITY IS:

YOUR WANT

DESIRE

NEED

WORTH

SURVIVAL

LIFE

YOU YOURSELF.

Chapter 9: Travelogue of life!

Life is a journey in which we all have some aims and goals which we want to achieve at the end of the day.

Setting a goal is as easy as making tea, everyone can do it, but turning it into reality is the real chase behind it.

If I tell you the recipe of a dish, YOU can easily make it, but will it taste the same like my one?

NO right?

Do YOU know why?

Because, there is always a motive behind it, hard work, emotion, passion, and a secret ingredient. The secret ingredient is always the dedication and love behind doing that work. Just like cooking is an art, so is life. We all know the colours which can make a rainbow, but how YOU put it down on the paper makes all the difference in life.

Many people think, life doesn't work on plan…

Let me ask YOU only,

What is a PLAN?

Or,

What is a G O A L?

Why is it necessary to have one?

Is it necessary to have one?

"Goal adds to the purpose of life, and gives us an aim to achieve in life."

Goal gives us the meaning of life, something to focus on, something to live for.

Each morning when YOU wake up, YOU have to know what YOU need to achieve, or plan what will YOU do the whole day.

Just setting a goal is easy, it takes just a minute, but it isn't the one-day decision and effort that makes the goal true, is the continuous effort given each day to one day, finally, achieving the goal.

YOU need to plan each day, do something for the goal, each day.

For example, if you wake up early in the morning and think, "I have nothing to do, so it's better I go back to sleep."

Is it wrong? NO, it may not be to you, because you don't have any reason to wake up, continue the day, to continue life…

A person who doesn't have any plan or goal, gets used to their comfort zone and that's how they live further, aimlessly and a boring life.

GOALS are one of the assets which determines our course of life, just big dreams like becoming a doctor, scientist, are not goals. Goals are every little small thing as well which we do in order to live life and sustain it.

For example, waking up in the morning is also a goal, brushing your teeth, having a bath, having breakfast, going to work, studies or anything important or doing something fun like drawing, dancing, everything is a goal you want to perform to finally end your day.

YOU not only plan for years later in life, but also a few minutes later in life as well.

Goal is not always about achieving a milestone, but it is just a word to determine YOU got what YOU wanted too.

For example, even the word SUCCESS itself may be a very strong word, but is of no value if YOU don't feel it. At times, we achieve so much and still don't feel the success and at times, we don't achieve some reward, but still feel we have succeeded. As a practical approach it is just a word which defines your achievement for You as well as the world.

Others can also empathise, sympathise, and guide You, but the journey is always yours, the life is always yours, and the goals are always yours.

YOU need to give your goal the importance it deserves in your life. YOU need to bring necessary changes in your life to achieve what You want to, make plans, target them and have it.

YOUR EACH DAY,

EACH HOUR

EACH MINUTE,

EACH SECOND, should count.

If YOU have no goal and waste each day, at the end, YOU will be the one to cry and say, "Life has offered me nothing."

In the race of life, YOU all have a journey, which is a mixture of everything you go through. In the end, YOU need to be proud of yourself, not by achieving your goal, but by knowing the fact that YOU did your hundred percent to achieve your goal.

That's what matters the most in life.

Let's get a moral type story…

Priti was a passionate soul, she loved to dance. Since the age of 4 she had been dancing. She always wanted to be a dancer and choreographer but as she grew up, she was told by her parents and society to choose a career option.

When she told her father that she wanted to be a dancer, he denied and said she won't be able to succeed. She tried to explain once, but he denied by telling, "Hear my advice, I am guiding you, I will always tell you for your good." Hearing this even she didn't argue and agreed to be a DOCTOR, as her father always wanted.

Finally, she became one, and by the age of 30, she was one of the renowned doctors in Dubai. She still wasn't happy after achieving so much. One day, when she saw her daughter dancing, she just saw her face and its smile, the sweat, everything reminded her of her old days, and she being ignorant started dancing with her. Behind her sweat, she thought her hard work is nothing.

YOU know why it happened?

She earned good, but her goal was not earning. Her father thought a good earning would satisfy her, and made her think as that is the goal, but money is just a medium to achieve happiness, it's not the happiness itself.

Because her true happiness was dancing.

That day, she danced as if a caged bird was free after a long time. That day her happiness knew no boundaries, she realised it was wrong of her not to accept her talent and ability and to not think she was capable and worthy of being a good dancer. She destroyed her goal and made her life meaningless.

What we understand as moral is that a person's earning and social status doesn't make them happy or satisfied. YOU are happy and satisfied only when you do something you wanted and aimed for.

Yes, we have to be open minded, accept other's thoughts, embrace them but then overpower it with our goals?

No, never…

If YOU have knowledge, your earning will never matter to YOU,

If YOU do something of what YOU love, you can never get tired of it.

Priti sacrificed her goal not for anyone else, but she was the one who wasn't sure of her own goal, and thought she won't be successful in it. She learned dance for 14 years and then just left her goal because she got impacted by her father and his words.

In life also, others will try to show you the way, they might be wrong or right, but at the end it's your goal, and you need to achieve it, and nobody else can feel the pain and happiness behind it.

...

We all heard the name of RATAN NAVAL TATA, the Industrialist, the person who makes his goals and visions come true. He knows what he wants to achieve, and also how.

It's not that he has some special powers or special people to do his work, he is a normal human like all of us. At 21, he made his companies growth up to 40% more. Long before he achieved it, he knew he would achieve it, because he made it happen. He doesn't have any Aladdin KA Jinn but it was his efforts towards his goals which made it happen. Even if he wouldn't have achieved it, people would have sympathised, or would have said, it's okay!

But, the fact that he knew it was not okay, made the change. He knew he had to do it, anyhow. His ethics have always inspired new entrepreneurs to come forward and achieve their goals as well. He makes his own journey!

Life offers everyone a chance to fulfil their goals, it's YOU who needs to think YOU are worthy enough and not just set your goals, but also work hard each day to fulfil them.

Your travelogue of life should inspire YOU to be better each day, for experience is the greatest teacher in the book of life, and YOU are the sole author of it.

We have to learn to accept ourselves, our talent, skills, goals just the way they are, and believe that we can achieve them.

We need to accept other's thoughts but be self-worthy at the same time.

In the travelogue of life, YOU are your own traveloguer and YOU have to write your life,

Your OWN WAY,

THAT DEFINES,

YOUR PLANS,

YOUR GOALS,

YOUR LIFE,

AND YOU!

Chapter 10: Choose Time so Time chooses You

TIME CREATES HISTORY.

Long before, when the world was full of jungle, nomads, our ancestors, i.e. prior to 1500 B.C., in Egypt, there was nothing like the concept of T I M E.

People used to measure time looking at the direction of the sun, moon and stars.

Can you even imagine that scenario?

After that people started measuring time as 60 minutes or even a minute using the sand glass or hour glass. The question which lies here is what was the need for people to measure time and work accordingly?

Why they even wanted to invent the concept of time, when the sun and moon positioning could easily tell them if it's day or night?

The reason was the fact that they knew the day needs to be divided in a schedule so that they can use it for their own benefit and have a comfortable life ahead.

They realized that the days need to be more concentrated, and each moment and hour needs to count so that people could work more efficiently by managing time.

When Babylonians invented the concept of " Division

of hour", people could divide the time into hours, as in there are 24 hours, and the concept of real time and time clock followed. That's how finally the 12 hour clock was invented, which when completed 1 full rotation denotes 12 hours of a day to be completed, followed by the next 12 hours to complete a whole day.

Even the concept of having breakfast in the morning, lunch in the afternoon, dinner at night within a time, was the invention which took place with the invention of time only.

In the same manner, the concept of day, week, month, and a year of 365 days on Earth came into existence, for there was a reason for humans to know the time and to act according to the time for their own benefit and to work systematically.

YOU might have read,

"Once upon a time…." or

"Ek baar ki baat hai…",

"Pehle ke zamane mein…"

That's exactly how people remember time and its events as…

Time changes people, brings the necessary change in people, their beliefs, their habits, their work, their fashion style, choice of foods, and so on.

YOU might just live in the moment and forget it all, but time captures all these moments with it, just as YOU grow each day, each moment, each second…

That's how time works or YOU can say it's the rule of time that once something has happened, it happened. There is no substitute to that moment or time once again in real life.

Just the second this line was written, even this line became a history.

If we look at the definition of time,

"Time is measured by all the actions which take place."

But in reality, it's the opposite. Time is just a measurement of our action which we do in our daily course, which is recorded in the tool of time, and which eventually leads to the concept of it being past, present and future.

That's how T I M E and Y O U travel.

B

U

T

Do YOU know, how to value time?

OF COURSE NOT!

Let's tell YOU, why as well…

Rahul was a successful Production Manager and had done MBA from a very renowned institution, and was well placed in a company. He had a handsome salary package, which somehow, he was proud of as well as satisfied it. He was of the concept that the amount he was getting was enough for his life sustenance, and that now he could relax for the next 5-6 years.

On the other hand, his friend rather colleague, Roshan, who was the Sales Manager in the same company, used to devote his time, along with his job, to his passion of writing, as well as tried each day to upgrade his skill in leadership qualities, public speaking, as well as learned English courses as well as French, for he knew his company wanted to expand their business in France as well in the near future. He didn't stick to his present time, but took efforts for the changes which would occur in future, and to manage them wisely. He even believed in the concept of investing, for he was wise to know the theory of compounding, and that the value of money would change with the change in time.

Exactly after 2 years, Rahul was nowhere in competition to Roshan, for he was the same monotonous with no new skill or art. When their company shifted to France, Rahul struggled in terms of knowing their language, their new machines as well as financially as the value of money had changed by that time.

On the other side, for Roshan everything went smooth, as he moulded himself with time.

Both had the same salary, same position, it just was the ability to value time that made a whole lot of difference in their future, as well as life!

Change was the essence, change was the need, and the one who doesn't accept time and its changes, loses it all in the race of life.

…

If YOU remember Harry Potter, one of the greatest series of all times, Hogwart's time travel was a tool used by Harry Potter and Hermoine and later Albus Severus Potter.

What the time-turner did was to rewind the clock, which put the 'weaver of the Time-Turner' in the past.

In Hogwarts world, time was controlled, the actions relayed, moments changed, time reversed.

But do YOU think, in the real world, YOU can reverse time, change your actions, control the and the actions which already took place? Save a person who died or bring a person back to life? Undo the words said, undo your mistakes, undo your moments, erase the past, erase all the bad memories and preserve the good ones?

If the same thing was to be told to the people in 15th Century, would they believe in the concept of existence of a place like Hogwarts, which controls time and had a time machine?

NO, right?

The question isn't that if Hogwarts exists, but the fact that with time, people's belief system changes and so do their habits.

For example, previously, when there was no concept of education, people didn't want their sons to even study, but rather grow up and handle their work instead. But now, when they saw the change education brought to society and people, they practiced going to school, learn things, and that's how the education system grew.

Even the fact of existence of mythological Gods like Krishna, Rama, and so on, was believed by people, when they saw and read about them via books, televisions shows, movies and so on. That's how their belief system grew.

…

In the end, it's always You who can work as per the time and make time your friend, and keep moving forward and plan yourself, your life as per the time.

Time has witnessed it all, the greatest inventions, revolution, discoveries…

Rather than time working with or without YOU, make time work for YOU.

If how is the question,

Here is the answer…

TIME can't undo your actions, but YOU can.

But when?

Before YOU MAKE IT HAPPEN.

And how?

By investing in time,

If YOU learn to plan things as per time, it can be your biggest healer as well as destructor.

It's as simple as this:

HAVE A GOAL,

PRIOTISE THINGS THAT ARE YOUR PRIORITY

HAVE A PLAN,

SCHEDULE THE PLAN IN YOUR LIFE

WORK AS PER YOUR PLAN

ACHIEVE YOUR GOAL

RULE OVER TIME!

Time is a tool, understand that there is no one like Doreamon who would have a *time machine* or an *anywhere door* that would lead YOU to your goal and destination.

After all, who decides your ultimate destination?

YOUR TIME?

NO

YOUR DESTINY?

NO, IT JUST DECIDES WHERE, NOT HOW.

Yes, destiny decides where life would lead YOU, but how your life is going to be is in YOUR OWN HANDS.

If YOU see mutual funds, share market, bonds, fixed deposit, all these require investment to give YOU future benefits, that also swhat YOU require. Just like in life, YOU need time to achieve your goals. Time, Patience and Goal is one of the deadliest combinations which is a life destructor as well as a blessing in disguise.

To make your life, you need a goal and to make that goal work, do you need luck?

No,

YOU need time in your favour.

YOU need patience.

YOU need to learn the art of managing things with time, multiple life, goals, people, only then YOU will succeed in bringing time in your favour.

All YOU need to learn is that,

If YOU don't choose the right time for YOU,

Time will not choose YOU, to be the real YOU, in the race of life.

So, make time work for YOU,

Work with YOU,

And, to choose YOU,

JUST THE WAY YOU WANT IT TO…

And, CHOOSE TIME OVER EVERYTHING,

SO THAT ONE DAY, TIME CHOOSES YOU TO BE THE ONE.

Chapter 11: Freedom - Financial, Mental and Emotional

The seven-letter word that everybody wants in their life is FREEDOM.

If I ask YOU what is freedom?

How will YOU define it?

Is the state of being free from making crucial choices, decisions or living in the society and the world without opinions or judgement called freedom?

If YOU say a Yes, then that's not freedom, that's a way of running from something that fears you, scares you, and restricts you from a part of the society.

Because, YOU don't want to be free.

YOU want to free of all your fears and have nothing to be free of.

Is that what freedom does to a person?

What exactly does freedom do?

When long back, during pre-independence, people were demanding freedom, I understand the reason. They didn't like to be caged and work for others or didn't want to be tortured.

That was freedom!

"The only real prison is fear and the only real freedom is freedom from fear."

- Aung San Suu Kyi

If YOU define freedom as having a choice of your own, to do things your way.

But again, even that's not what freedom is. That's like having it my way, as per my comfort, the easy, smooth and happening way.

Emotional attachments generate fear, either we are born with it or it generates with time.

We all experience this when we want something and we don't get that. We change as a human, we start to get angry, complain about it, and we suffer internally as well with that, for we fear that someone has it and we don't.

This is what the fear of fear does. YOU all fear something and the entire life you all struggle to get to your own comfort zone, leaving all your issues and struggles behind.

I have seen people having the fear of something their entire life. Some people have the fear of water, height, darkness but one fear YOU all have inside is the fear of being judged.

But fear is not just about self, you cannot overcome your fear without other human interaction. You need to discuss your fear with your family, friends or anyone you want to, who can handle you and tell you what fears you, why it does and how you can be healed.

It's just that mental and emotional support, to help us be courageous enough to fight it.

Fear is the path to the Dark Side. Fear leads to anger, anger leads to hate, hate leads to suffering.

-Yoda

A human's fear changes with their age.

When we are a children, we fear the fact that if our homework if not done, the teacher will scold us or if we break something, our parents will scold us.

When we grow older, we fear about studies that if we don't get this much marks or don't get into this college, our life will be affected.

When we grow more older, fear of job, promotion and then after being a parent, fear of our child's life not being in danger, or giving them a good life, their responsibilities fear us.

When we grow old, diseases fear us, the care for our children and their life and problems fear us.

In each stage fear is there and will always be. That's how the cycle works and humans grow and change.

To be in fear or be fearless, we need humans, emotions and someone to calm us.

If you have fear of public speaking, you can't let it go.

Maybe you need to start speaking in front of the mirror, then around four to five people and then gradually on the stage one day. There are various courses which help people gain confidence and practice their fear to overcome it.

But again, you want to get free of this fear, because you fear that if you don't get rid of it, in life you will be left behind, because someday you need to speak on stage as well. So, you again want to be free of one fear, for some other fear that captures you.

To be free is a choice, so is to beat the fear.

The ONLY WAY to be free is to target your fear,

KNOW WHAT FEARS YOU

WHY IT FEARS YOU

HOW IT FEARS YOU…

Just like Sachin Tendulkar, what if he would not have given up studies or questioned himself that, "What if I won't be successful at cricket?"

He overcame his fear, for he had to do something in life, and academics was not the road to it. So, he prioritized something and the fear of not failingin cricket was what made him practice cricket the whole day, so that one day he would achieve his target of playing for India.

Even he was not fearless, just when people appreciated him for his talent, he got COURAGE to do something.

…

FREEDOM from the cage of society is important as well. Giving up your dreams in the name of financial burden or fear of financial problems is another fear which haunts YOU for a lifetime, because the rest of your life YOU regret being feared.

When YOU fear something, people make YOU fear of it more. They use it as an advantage, like fear of God, fear of religions, fear of tantra-mantra, shrap…

The fact of being free itself, is a thing to be feared. For a human brain to work and be disciplined, it can be free of all burdens financially or emotionally.

For example, a very small but powerful change I witnessed myself.

One of my friends, Sanjana, feared cockroaches since her childhood. Whenever she used to see one, she would run away to the bed, scream aloud and make a scene.

As she grew, her fear grew stronger. She never found the reason to overcome it, nor did she ever do it herself.

When she became a mother, she went through certain changes. One day, when her daughter was playing, she suddenly saw a cockroach and the 5-year-old kid started to cry out aloud. Seeing her cry and being feared, Sanjana ran to her daughter, held the cockroach with her own hands and threw it out of the window.

Suddenly, her fear went.

Suddenly in one day, did a miracle happen?

NO, she found a reason to overcome her fear, and then she became more powerful.

She understood the fear, but now, it was not about her getting self-empowered and being fearless for her, but she had someone in her life.

Her fear just changed, from she being feared of a cockroach, now she feared the fact that her daughter should not be harmed or get into danger by anyway.

We all fear something and that fear is what people take advantage of, and use against us in our life. For example, if someone has hydrophobia, other people like friends or family might scare that person, against that fear, so that he/she listens to them. But once that person becomes free of their fear, they become so powerful and strong that no one can break them.

It is humans who tell us what we fear and who give us the courage to fight our fears.

Fear is good, but overcoming it is what makes YOU a human. Turn your fear into your strength, invest in your fear, so that finally one day, it becomes your POWER!

At the end, freedom is not financial, but emotional and mental as well. When your mind doesn't fear anything for, 'IT'S ALL IN THE MIND'.

But now, when each one of us wishes to get freedom.

It's nothing, FREEDOM HAS BECOME AN ILLUSION.

We all want it, ignorant of the fact from what something that has captured us or something that fears us, And only YOU can attain your freedom. There is no person who is living without fear, some fear losing people, some fear of crime, rape, some fear robbery, terrorists, some fear of their flaws coming out to the world, their lies being caught, their wrong actions being disclosed and so on.

The mark that fear leaves, stays for a lifetime. Therefore, it's good to fear, to value things, fear is important but not when it captures your life, your journey and bounds YOU around it and tortures YOU mentally.

YOU need to know yourself, your fear, what fears YOU and how YOU can overcome it.

It's not a one-night transformation, but a slow and beautiful one to get out of your fear zone. YOU know yourself best, as well as your fears, as well as the real reason behind the fear.

In life, our big fear at times overcomes our small fears. Fear is always there, it just that we get rid of small ones because a big one becomes more powerful, and this is how by taking baby steps, you don't become fearless but POWERFUL enough.

YOU JUST CHANGE YOUR FEAR,

WITH CHANGE IN TIME AND LIFE SITUATIONS...

The target must not be to be fearless, or get freedom, but to be Courageous!

To get the power, to face your fear.

...

There is no escape to fear, to attain freedom. Freedom is nothing but an illusion, for YOU yourself don't know what exactly YOU want to be free of. YOU don't want to be free, YOU want to be powerful, fearless, so that no one can subjugate your thoughts, your respect, your opinion, your head, and YOU.

Here, I remember few lines of Mr. Tagore:

"Where the mind is without fear and the head is held high, where knowledge is free.

Where the world has not been broken up into fragments by narrow domestic walls.

Where words come out from the depth of truth, where tireless striving stretches its arms toward perfection.

Where the clear stream of reason has not lost its way into the dreary desert sand of dead habit.

Chapter 12: SELF, Service and Community

LOG KYA KAHENGE!

The biggest disaster we all do and fall in the trap of is society!

What society will say changes us as a human in our every action. As each action has its own consequences, but sadly society doesn't bear the consequences with you directly, but you always do, for it's your life that affects in the whole game.

I

ME

& YOU...

Is there any difference?

NO, as YOU are ME, who is I.

BUT,

BUT,

BUT

YOU,

FAMILY

SOCIETY

WORLD

Now, is there any difference?

Of course, there is.

YOU are a part of the society, family and world, and YOU make them all.

For example, your identity is what defines you, your personality is what builds you and that's how you present yourself in the real world.

The people and society may just mould you in their way, but it can never overcome what you really are from inside.

There is always an individuality in each one of us, which makes us different.

Today, if we look at powerful people, for example, SANDEEP MAHESHWARI, the motivational speaker.

If you listen to his speeches, you will realize, he doesn't say something new or different from what we know. For example, in one of his sessions, he told that if you fear something, practice that thing every day.

Did he say something we don't know?

Its just that because he said it, it created an IMPACT.

He is not a millionaire or a very powerful person, nor does he tell you a secret mantra for success in life. It's just that he has a personality that people look up to in their life, for seeking motivation.

Another strong personality like A.P.J Abdul Kalam, we

all know him, love him and are inspired by him. Was he successful?

Maybe yes, because if he was the President, but actually he was an inspiration in the lives of many. He was the reason scientists got such a supreme position in India, and was able to develop quality education in the scientific department in India. It happened because he changed it, and how, by creating an impact with his actions. He was such a powerful personality. If you ask yourself, you might say yes, he was famous as well as successful.

But to him, maybe he wasn't, for he always tried to achieve something new and his last motive as written in his book, was to empower knowledge to all places in India, making India a developed country by 2020. He couldn't achieve it, because he died.

For each person in life, successful has an altogether different perception and parameter. You might be successful but not famous. There are many people out there, like our soldiers, who have a dream to fight for India and die for India.

The ones who get martyred die with pride, because they are successful in their mission, but were they famous or very rich?

On the other hand, a person might be very famous but not successful. Also, a person has different measures of it as well. Like a dancer who might be very famous and successful in life winning many awards, achievements and so on, but maybe his personal success which he treats as one, would be to win an International dance competition, or to fly a plane someday and so on.

A person cannot be successful for everyone as well, like an actor might be very successful in his career, but may have failed in his real-life role as a husband, father or son. So, is he successful for his family too?

You cannot succeed in every place, relation and sector, but your life can always impact someone else's life. Like, for some people, when they see their parents struggling, that itself becomes an inspiration to them, which creates an impact in their life, for which they set their goal to achieve something.

The teachers who teach us in school, they are people who change our life, create an impact, give us knowledge to become something great in life.

When you get famous, even they get successful to give you the power and knowledge to become one.

In society, a person can always be famous in wrong or right ways. If someday, you run away from your house, or get kidnapped, you get famous, isn't it?

You might be financially very rich, successful and famous, but that doesn't make you? and powerful for the world. Like Vijay Malaya, today he is so powerful and famous but is he an inspiration or has he created any impact positively in our life?

Will you tell your kid anyway to become like him?

On the other hand, Ratan Tata, who is also very famous, is the one who holds the power to change the world, and no one can question him.

Today, if he passes a statement that he wants to do something for his company, the other moment all the businessmen would follow the same. WHY?

Because they trust him, his decision and that is what his power is, that he inspires people.

In society as well, each one is different. If you have four friends, they all have different qualities and features that inspire you in some or the other way. One might be the one with whom you can share your life issues, one might be the one with whom you can enjoy or comedy type, one might be the one who always demotivates you or tells you the harsh reality, and one might always just give you positive vibes and help you.

Each person holds a place, and is someone you cannot replace with someone else in life.

The society is what we make of it.

You need to make your place with your goals, targets, opinions, personality, identity and create a powerful impact in the lives of people.

Your knowledge, skills and goals are what is the strength which makes you grow in life.

Success is just a name given when you achieve something, but the day you feel you have achieved something is the day you get successful, irrespective of whether the society feels it or not.

Your work and service to the society is what makes your place in people's life and changes the community.

Your knowledge will always matter in life.

There is no complex equation in it, The strengthening part in the equation needs to have a balance with the learning part, so that YOU can adapt to the changes in life, accept them, cope up with them.

Knowledge is the key which is exponential in its nature, which make all the equations right, which might seem complex but is one of the simplest equations which interlinks the entire journey of life…

Nothing is complex nor linear in the journey of life, it's all exponential, which is never ending, but YOU are the constant 'y' upon which the whole equation of x depends and stands for.

The day 'y' in the equation of life becomes undefined, the whole equation becomes undefined.

NLP

(Author insert here)

We have to live in the society and change it. For some people encourage us and some demotivate us, but they are all a part of the community you live in…

…

If YOU remember, when we started with the Chapter 1, we talked about YOU, and now in the end also we are talking about YOU. For YOU are someone, I can never forget or ignore. Everything I write today, is part of ME, who is also YOU.

YOU make the world, even before the world makes YOU what YOU are today.

In the world of YOU, YOU are not just the beginning and the end, but the centre as well.

No matter what experience life has provided YOU, what age group YOU belong too,

I as an author want YOU to take my lines and words as a guide, to have a life YOU can be proud of. YOU may not achieve the moon, but the stars are always there for YOU.

In the entire book, I have highlighted the word YOU, to tell YOU, that nothing matters before YOU in the world.

Service before self is old,

Now it has to be, **YOU above all.**

In the end, all I can say to YOU is that I am one of YOU, writing it to YOU, to tell YOU, that YOU are important before everyone else.

Saari Zindagi mein tere liye jiya,

Aur jab gaya, to ye malal rahe gaya, ki kya jiya bhi toh kya jiya...

YOU ARE IMPORTANT,

YOU ARE STRONG

YOU ARE YOU,

BE THE REAL YOU,

YOU ARE BEAUTIFUL!

JUST THE WAY YOU ARE,

AND, BE PROUD OF BEING YOU!

Epilogue

Since times unknown, there is a dilemma in human thoughts and beliefs, more evident than the egg and chicken causality. It causes the clash of need to blend in with others and create a unique famed identity...

It's a massive issue, and it was something I put a finger on as a child, and struggled through my formative years and have found a few simple practices that can set the dilemma to a process to enhancement and empowerment with support...

The problem statement is massive and diverse, yet a few simple practices done with discipline can clear all limiting beliefs and set an individual on the way to his/her success. I started training people since my high school, via tuitions, where I used to get them hands on my computer (though that was not in the scope of the class), and always have taken an extra step to enhance the quality of one's life. As a dentist, a clinical researcher and trainer; on each role I have always taken extra effort to guide one for a better quality of life which has sometimes been a hit to my pocket too...

Now with the absolute formula to self-empowerment, I want to share my knowledge with one and all and via this book, I present a written guide that will set the reader on the path of self-assessment and re-discover the power in self.

It is not in scope of a single book to cover it all hence, there are many more on the way!!

About the author

Each one of us has a personality, an identity by which we present ourselves to the world.

Dr Sumana Chakraborty is one such woman, who has been playing multiple roles in her life relating to her skills and talents, to explore all she knows, and believes to pour it in her book of guide.

Dr Sumana is from Kolkata and a registered Dentist, clinical research professional, and Certified Trainer as well as a passionate dancer. She is an MBA professional and has been an entrepreneur since 2018. She has corporate experience in TCS, Cognizant and worked with pharma clients; Amgen and AbbVie. She loves to help and guide people to put their best foot forward in her venture named AskSarathi, which she co-founded with the aim of providing a better learning and writing service.

Dr Sumana, an atheist, believes that there is nothing greater than human strength, skills and capabilities. She highly values time and believing in living each moment happily with a smile, and practices smiling with good memories in bad times. She has been a friend, mentor, guide to all her friends, students, trainees, and family, and is always ready to help people and bring moments of happiness to every life she touches. She prefers to isolate in times of grief, being a natural introvert and that has seeded her power in finding self-strength for self, family and then community.

Having faced multiple anxiety issues due to incidents in her life, and have been in betrayals multiple times, she has learnt to be able to get up every time she falls, and essentially to lose the fear of falling and keep walking, crawling and steadily taking life to multiple goals of success. Celebrating each successful milestone and making the best of each day forms the base values of her life travelogue.

Her real-life situations and challenges have made her what she is today. She has very few people to count on in her life, like her close friends and family to whom she dedicates her entire life. She has always tried being a counsellor and listened to other's problems and issues, but has always restricted herself to the outside world. One would never find her discussing her issues, for she had always kept others ahead in life, in fact, each morning she gets out of bed with the motto to serve the society.

To know about her social life, one can read her thoughts and connect to her on

LinkedIn: www.linkedin.com/in/drsumana